My Perfect Partner

OPPOSITES THAT BECAME ONE

ANTHONY VANDYKE

Opposites

That became ONE

My Perfect Partner

"A book about love and
honor in marriage"

GRATUITY

Gratuity
Direct Number: 2134389957
(888) 290-0987
9350 Wilshire Blvd, Suite 203,
Beverly Hills, CA 90212

Published by Gratuity: 10/03/2024

ISBN: 978-1-965386-10-1(sc)
ISBN: 978-1-965386-11-8(e)

Table of Contents

Special Thanks

Special thanks to all the people who supported me through the rough patches adjusting to a new life without the love of my life. January 24, 2024 started a new journey for both of us. Even though we are not physically together, we still connect daily in the spirit. I can still hear Nikki say things that I am doing right and doing wrong.

New Community, you are the best church in the world.

Brenda Blake, you are a good mother, with a caring heart. Thanks for accepting me as your son-in-law. Now I am your third son; God has a sense of humor.

The Philly crew, much love to you, Conrad, Saafie, Judy, Shanell, Felecia, and the other crew thanks for loving on me and answering my phone calls.

Dr. Stephen Patterson thanks for answering my phone calls and listening. Sometimes you just want a person to listen and not respond.

The VanDyke Crew, you did your thing, you rallied behind me to ensure I was good. Mom thanks for your unconditional love, Tyrone thanks for being the big brother, Paulette thanks for always asking me if I'm good and Rodney, thanks for answering my calls late in the evening. Your different time zone gave me a few extra hours to chat with you.

My Pastor, Dr. R.A. Vernon, you stopped your schedule to listen and help navigate through the immediate things that needed care after the passing of Nicole. In addition, you rallied the shepherd connection, they are still calling and texting, it does not go unnoticed.

Bishop Rosie S. Oneal, when you showed up my heart exploded knowing you were there, thanks for being there when I needed you most.

Dr. Larry Mitchell, thanks for being my sound board. You listened and agreed with me, never rushing to judgement as I was pouring out thoughts about the soon masterpiece.
LOL

OPPOSITES CONNECTED

Nicole	_Anthony_
City Girl	Country Boy
Super Smart Student	Below Average
Super Conservative Taker	Risk
Ask Questions	Assume Answers
Investigate Value	Take at Face
Checking You Out Waving You In	Always
Serious	Always Smiling
Slender at Birth	Chunky at Birth
Going Above and Beyond Enough	Doing Just
Realist	Dreamer
Facts	Feelings

As we grew together our differences merged, and we became one in many areas of our lives. We grew together because we liked, loved and respected how different we were. Nicole and I were the perfect match. We were like peanut butter and jelly.

Opposites That Connected

It was August 1994, when I saw Nicole Gaynelle Blake for the first time, and I knew she was my forever lover and soon best friend. Though I knew quickly that she was the one, not so much for Nicole. Our glaring differences made our relationship so special. I was what she needed, and she was what I needed and more. Honestly, I never thought in a million years that love could be so beautiful. Our love was so organic. I found my soul mate before I knew what a soulmate was. Amazing how God, gives us what we need, before we even recognize the void in our lives.

It was love at first sight for me. I was fresh off the road from being a traveling salesperson, now located in a corporate office setting. Early one morning with my back against the wall I saw Nicole walking by my window, headed to her new office. My heart jumped as she gracefully walked by. Several mornings went by and I waited patiently to see her gracefully pass my office. Not sure about the initial conversation, I eventually got my nerves together and we connected.

I remember getting her number. That very first call on the pay phone we talked for hours about nothing; we had meaningful conversations. Did you notice I said, my initial call was on a pay phone, no working house phone or cell phone? Little did I know my life was about to take a turn for the better.

Something was different about Nicole; I remember saying to myself. I had finally connected with a college girl that knew who she was. One day Nicole asked me to pick up lunch for her and a coworker, it wasn't much more than $20. I went to the restaurant and didn't have enough money to cover the charge, embarrassed that I was broke. I immediately went to coach Buggs, my former high school football coach, to borrow the money. I dashed back to the restaurant to pick up the food.

Nicole said thanks, she ate the lunch, and we talked later that evening. Meanwhile, I didn't know Nicole had called the restaurant, and they told her I didn't have enough money. It was sometime later I discovered she knew I had financial problems, but she gave me the chance to prove what a real man I could be. Wow.

I had to get it together because she saw something in me that I didn't see in myself. I had no good reason to be broke. My life just needed order and discipline. We went on to date exclusively, and it got serious quickly. I knew I wanted to spend the rest of my life with her.

Remember, I am a country boy from Smithfield, Virginia, super trusting and always smiling. Nicole was a beautiful, smart accountant from north Philadelphia. Nicole was a graduate of Bodine High School of International Affairs; a place where smart people went. Nicole realized what she wanted to be at an early age. She realized if you worked hard, did your best, life would produce the results you needed.

In so many ways we were opposite people, her environment caused her to be cautious with people, guarded and very aware of her surroundings. This was foreign to me. I didn't grow up in Mayberry, but I trusted all people and was too accommodating in many cases. My philosophy caused turmoil many times, because we saw life from two different lenses. This glaring difference had advantages, nevertheless we needed each other's perspective, because it made us the unique couple that we became.

After we got married, I noticed I was different than any man Nicole dated. All the brothers before me had a different stature, over 6 feet tall and slim build. I was... One day I gathered myself and asked the question, "why did you pick me?" Nicole paused and said, ""You are a good person, kindhearted and a provider that will always work hard." She got that information from a person that knew my family. Now that I look back, her answer made sense. Nicole knew what she wanted to build, and I happened to be the right person to help her get it done. Nicole saw in me what I

didn't see in myself. She constantly told me, "Once you realize who you are, you will be unstoppable." Honey, I must say, I see it now. Wow.

The life we built together was amazing and still growing. Nicole, you gave me the foundation to soar, your boy is going to make you proud.

The Boy That Became a Man

I can honestly say, I was a good boy who became a man over time. The problem with modern marriages is that they don't leave room to grow or create a path to become a better version of yourself.

How ironic the musical group, Boyz II Men, are from Philadelphia. That is exactly what I became over 30 years that Nicole and I were together. We were married for nearly 28 and 1/2 years, and it didn't take me long to know that Nicole Gaynelle would become my wife.

I made a lot of mistakes during the first years of our marriage. Let's get the record clear, I never cheated or was ever tempted in that manner. My mistakes were due to my boyish tendencies and not being willing to accept responsibility for the boneheaded things I did. I was a people pleaser which is not good when you are called by God to cling to your wife and forsake all others (Gen. 2:24; Eph 5:31). Nicole and I never had a problem with each other, and it was always other people that I allowed to cause confusion in our young marriage.

The boy in me needed healing, I am not sure why I always cared about what people thought about me, which made me a people pleaser. Often, I would make decisions to help people financially that put our personal finances in jeopardy.

Specifically, I remember spending over fifty thousand dollars of a line of credit we had on our home. Nicole had no knowledge of what I did. I didn't have a drug problem or a side chick. I was being nice and wanting people to be happy with me. I wanted to be the person that solved problems for others, which is not a good thing for any marriage relationship.

There came a time when we needed the money, and I had to tell her the truth that all the money was gone. I broke her heart, and Nicole cried for weeks about the betrayal. I felt the disappointment she had in me. At that moment I realized

I did a very bad thing and needed to fix me. Well, how do you fix spending that kind of money and not getting permission from the person that loved me and had my back. The boy in me rose up and said, it was my money too, rather than admitting I was wrong.

It took me a while to come to grips that this caused a rift in our relationship. The awesome thing about Nicole is she never exposed me to the world, she continued to love me and build me up. When I say build me up, she made me accountable for my actions. It takes a special person to forgive and still love unconditionally. Never would always remind me of my financial mismanagement. I couldn't understand why she continued to mind me after we recovered financially. I know the reason now, some things we do are deep rooted and take time to get out of our system. Guys please understand, recovery takes a long time, sometimes. The reason I said guys, we are most often full of machoism, and it takes time for the boy to become a man. I was fortunate Nicole knew how to help and not stunt her own growth. It's important that partners understand their struggles because if not attended to, the struggles hinder the marriage. A healthy marriage is the result of two people willing to grow and fix problems, so the problems become teaching moments for others to see and benefit from.

I was no longer trustworthy when it came to finances. How ironic that I worked in the financial industry but wasn't a good steward of my personal finances. Nicole separated her money from mine and made me responsible for the mortgage and other large ticket items. She didn't want excuses only the money to pay those bills. Nicole didn't care if it took every dime I had, it was a lesson I needed to learn. The boy needed discipline and accountability. People will change when those close to them hold them to a high standard and demand that they be better.

I wanted my marriage and was willing to do what it took to make things right. What I soon discovered was I was a public success and a private failure. If I didn't change, our marriage would have no chance of survival. Nicole was the first principal-driven person I knew, there was no deviation from the truth no matter the person or situation. It took nearly two decades to understand the importance of being principal-driven.

Below is a blog, www.anthonyinspiration.com, that I wrote in honor of Nicole. She is the most principal-driven person I know.

Principal People

They never compromise the truth; they are ok with you being upset with them.

Why is taking the position of truthfulness important?

One reason only, the truth always prevails.

Now that I am older, I see what they saw. I am slowly becoming one of them because of the success I have seen in their lives.

Principal people view life as black or white, there is no gray with them.

Principal people do not break rules because they understand the consequences of being rogue.

How do you identify principal people?

They are Confident.

They are Cautious.

They are Conservative.

They are Concise.

They are Caring.

I challenge you to change your life narrative, become principal driven. People will take notice and begin to trust you more than ever before. Doors will open and opportunities will seek you, as the aroma of being a principal person drips from your pores.

Written by Anthoy VanDyke www.anthonyinspiration.com

The second lesson the boy learned is that the job isn't finished until it is finished. Nicole would never leave things undone. I saw her stay up until 2am getting reports done for work and church. Nicole understood the importance of delivering what you promised.

I remember two weeks before she passed, I propped her up in the hospital chair to complete the year end closing. Nicole worked for an international construction company, the year-end reporting needed to happen, and she continued to complete her assignment being deathly ill. Nicole was extremely sick, but she understood the importance of not leaving people hanging. After she completed the year end closing, she never turned her computer on again. Drop the mic!!! Nicole knew the end was near on earth and soon, the beginning of a new journey.

Most men enter marriage with a level of immaturity that must be erased to become the husband God designed him to become. A mature spirit happens over time, when you live beyond your own personal needs and desires. Nicole, my perfect partner, made sure I was good in every area of my life.

Now that Nicole is here in spirit only, I know the importance of getting things done in a timely manner. Sleep comes later but getting the job done is important. Men are fragile boys waiting for instructions on how to be that provider and protector. I have discovered this scares men in today's society. Being that provider and protector means you must die to yourself so others you love are good. My heart breaks when I see a couple about to bring children into the world and the father is still a boy mentally. Physically he was able to procreate, but he is not ready to be a father. Sorry I am on another tangent, back to Nicole.

The last months of Nicole's life required me to be her caretaker. What an honor to take care of my beautiful wife. I never saw it as a duty but a privilege that someone trusted me enough to take care of them.

Are you trustworthy? Who would trust you with their life and know that you would not drop the ball? Only men can be trusted. Boys run from the challenge as they find another field to play in while those, they should be assisting are left to fend for themselves. The tough times define character and commitment, these are the days of love. Real men do it without expectation and acknowledgment.

Nicole, I thank you for loving me through my inconsistent behaviors, faults and failures. I am the man I am today, because you loved me despite me. You saw what I could become before I realized what I needed to be. Finally, the boy has become a man!!!

Learning to LOVE Through Pain

You don't realize how much you love a person until you have those times. At the climax of Nicole's illness there was nothing I could do to soothe her pain. Nicole had a high tolerance for pain; she was able to move forward and smile without letting people know how she really felt.

When the person you adore is hurting, you hurt also. During those times I developed a quirky sense of humor to get Nicole distracted from the continual pain she faced for the last two years of her life. We hurt and ached together; it was our journey.

I didn't know love could go so deep. Love requires you to sometimes forget you even have needs. Love forces you to become what the other person needs. Love only wants to see that person better. Love is not something you can put on a timer; it becomes what is needed at that time.

I remember Nicole telling me how proud she was of me for taking care of her. I never saw it as taking care of her, it was simply loving the person God had given me to take care of. As a matter of fact, we took great care of each other.

We worked hard on trying to find out what each other needed and doing it for each other without being told to. Any time I mentioned needing clothing, Amazon would deliver the package within days. She cared about me and wanted me to be the best version of myself. Our love was much different than many other couples, because most people do it for show. Our love was real, and only we needed to see it. We didn't care what others thought, we were Bonnie and Clyde, we were each other's ride or die, literally.

As long as we knew how we felt about each other, it didn't matter what people said. We were the perfect, opposite couple built to change the world. Even with the passing of Nicole, together we are still making an impact on this generation and generations to come. God was able to trust us financially because we knew the importance of sowing seeds in the earth.

Pain in relationships is needed, because it drives out the selfish mindset we all possess. You don't know how selfish you are until someone needs all the love you can give. Love indeed conquers and covers all. I know we are taught to move on, but when you really love a person, you honor them while they are present and even more during their departure.

If you are in a relationship, be willing to love through the pain of indifference. Learn to love when you are tired and frustrated. Learn to love, when you feel like you have nothing valuable to give. Learn to love, when you don't feel like you are talking or expressing your dissatisfaction with your partner. Notice I said learn to love through those challenges we all face. The tough times are the defining moments of each relationship. Stop being so selfabsorbed that you miss what your spouse really needs and desires. Most men assume they know what their wives want and need, but they don't.

Brothers be better and learn your wife. Love your wife unconditionally because being present doesn't mean you cherish her. Ladies, I need you to stand your ground and not let him treat you like a spare tire, only when he needs you. You are precious and special, know it and demand it.

Nicole taught me a valuable lesson about being present in the moment, she desired my best and got my best. If she called, I tried never to let the phone ring more than twice because she needed to know she was always my number one.

Because we experienced the pain together, we were in love to the very end. I loved kissing her bald head, after the chemotherapy took her hair. Her pain became my pleasure to love without complaining because Nicole deserved to be loved. I encourage you to love harder, it will make a difference in the lives of the people you love most.

The Trials

The beautiful thing about being one is handling trials. Every marriage has trials, and some people are better at navigating through the murky waters than others.

Nicole and I can honestly say we seldom had problems with each other. It was outside noise that caused most of the division we faced. When we first met there was opposition on both sides of our families, and we pushed through the noise and made a better life together. We knew enough about each other to make it work. She accepted my weakness, and I loved her strength and determination. You will understand why, later.

In this chapter I will unveil a few things we grew together through. Notice I said grew together, not just going through life together. There is a big difference when you grow through trials, not just go through trials. Our trials are designed to make us strong provided we buckle up and learn from the turbulence. As a pastor I have observed marriage partners constantly pointing fingers rather than taking ownership for the problems they face.

The first trial we faced as a marriage couple was raising my child, we had before our marriage. It really wasn't a trial. It was a major situation we had to attack, to save our marriage. We both brought children into the marriage, and I was a proud happy father.

I want to emphasize the problem with having children outside marriage is not the children. The children are innocent bystanders for the situation consenting adults put them in. If you are a single person reading this book, try not to have children with people you have not committed to in marriage, because it greatly affects the children. I understand things happen and baby mama dream is real.

I remember like it was yesterday, Nicole asked me to get a paternity test. We needed to know the truth to structure our family on solid ground.

Nicole went through unnecessary drama with my child; because my child's mother didn't care for my new wife. The child will listen to their biological mother and dislike the wife, and not know why. Children only know what the parents tell them. Also notice I said child, I would never what to embarrass the child or their mother with writing this book. It doesn't matter if it was a boy or girl, the child is lovely and precious.

Nicole was a trooper, and she continued to love the child, while wondering if this was my biological offspring. The tension was strong; I was torn, causing Nicole to leave me briefly. I believe she went to a hotel to gather herself and give me room to make the right decision.

I wanted my marriage very bad, therefore I went through the court system to order a paternity test. I was able to order a paternity test because I was paying child support as responsible fathers do. Even though I was paying child support I provided for the child beyond what the court required; that's what real fathers do.

Several months later the test came back, and I was heartbroken to get the result. The person who I was proud to be called their father was not my biological child. I wanted to still be in their life, but things didn't work the way I planned them. I can honestly look at myself in the mirror and know I did my best with the situation and information given to me.

What I learned from this situation, I needed to forsake all others and make my wife first after my relationship with God. We must learn to trust the judgment of the person we have vowed to love and honor. This trial made me stronger as a person and gave me the needed resolve. Deep down we all knew the truth but chose not to acknowledge the truth.

My second glaring trial is intimacy. It's not what you think, I was a broken person with self-esteem and internal brokenness only God could repair. I thought sexual intimacy from my wife would cure my brokenness, it didn't. There were things I needed that only God could fix. I remember wanting more from Nicole and when I didn't get what I thought I needed, an internal explosion would take place from within. It never got violent, but I can remember saying things to her that weren't necessary.

Broken people hurt people; God had to heal me from within. Marriage was never designed to repair broken people;

this was something God had to do. Once I recognized my brokenness was a God problem our intimacy increased. Stop wanting people to fix your brokenness and take it to God!

I had to learn to value the queen God had given me. Men, we want to blame our spouses for our emptiness. It is not another person's responsibility to make us feel like a man. The boy must come to grips with being a man, if not, much hurt will come upon all those you love and cherish. This bleep in our young marriage could have gone another way, but because Nicole was able to process the entire situation, we were able to navigate once again through the storm. Lesson learned. You must love yourself first. When you understand your value, you understand we all have problems and must be willing to put the work in.

I didn't have the instruction guide to becoming the model husband. My father was a provider, but there were things I couldn't model him as a husband. On the other hand, there were things he taught me as a man that caused Nicole to fall and stay in love with me. He taught me the importance of hard work and being present in your family. Our marriage needed that because I was the first stable man Nicole had in her life. Wow, that was heavy. This is why I wrote this book to be a guide to help someone navigate through the murky waters of marriage.

The third trial was money. Man, I am still lucky to be alive. If you haven't noticed yet most of the boneheaded things that happened in our marriage came from me. At this point we just had built a second home. It was an awesome two story, home with a pond and ducks right next to our lot. We felt like George Jefferson, we made it.

We both had great jobs at the time. Nicole was doing very well; I had just discovered real estate. We had more money than we ever thought we would have. I remember flying to Houston Galleria just to go shopping. It was nothing to pay a bag for $3,000 and purchase a ring for $5,000. Nothing was too much for my wife and best friend. At this time in the early 2000's Nicole was balling; I was balling, and we were buying and flipping properties. We had more money than we ever had, life was good.

No one told me during the recession that would happen in 2008, the US economy turned, people were losing jobs, businesses were closing every day, and people were getting laid off. As I said earlier, I am the glass-always-halffull-guy, always believing I can make it happen and it will get better. I was the ultimate optimist in every situation which could be dangerous.

Someone should have told me more money brings more problems, As I said earlier, I wanted people to like me and think I was successful. I am not making excuses for my decision; I take all the blame. Meanwhile, my business tapered off, but my spending continued to escalate as if nothing had changed. I remember taking money from a savings account Nicole had to cover household expenses because I wasn't man enough to let her know I was broke. Then I started tapping into our home equity line of credit. Let's be honest I spent 60k from the line of credit without Nicole's permission. Nicole had no reason not to trust me, we had never faced financial hardship in our marriage.

A few months later Nicole got laid off, but she was okay because she had prepared for tough times since she was the financially responsible partner. I had to break the news to Nicole we had no equity left because I spent it all. My financial mismanagement started a tsunami of things, loss of credit, lowered credit scores, repossession of my Mercedes, and near foreclosure of our home. This was not a pretty situation, and I put us in a bad position financially.

It happened again; Nicole left me for the second time. She couldn't stay away long because we only had her 401k to live off. Notice I said, we only had her 401k. I was broke, busted and disgusting in my own eyes. Eventually she came back and started the process of forgiving me but vowed to separate her funds because she would never let me put her in that position again.

It got very bad financially. Our house went into foreclosure, my Mercedes was repossessed, and I was broke. Eventually, Nicole landed another job, not paying as much as the previous one, but it was enough that we could stay afloat. I struggled for years finding solid work.

Not many people survived the financial storm we faced. I caused much heartache with the money. Eventually I started to mature and recognize I had to do better. Nicole continued to love me and not expose my flaws to the world. I didn't deserve Nicole; she saw in me what I didn't see in myself. We survived the storm, got back on our feet financially and continued to build a great life together.

July 15, 2021, Nicole and I moved into her dream home that we built from the ground up. She designed every detail and was proud to call it home. The lesson learned is don't try to impress people. Fix yourself and learn to say no. When you say no, it helps you and them. People that can't say no have internal issues that need repair.

Saying no, only happens when you learn to love yourself. I am amazed at the baggage we carry into adulthood. On the outside we look solid and together, but on the inside, we are a hot mess. God is a healer, if you allow Him, He will fix your brokenness.

The Good Times

The good times Nicole and I shared were amazing. We were the perfect pair, wanting to see the world. It all started with our honeymoon. We were given a trip by Nicole's father to Paradise Island, Bahamas. We didn't know what to expect, but we loved what we saw.

It felt good leaving the United States for the first time, being in the Caribbean with my new bride. We didn't have much money; I caught a taxi to the local shops, eating island cuisine and enjoying the music. At that point we realized traveling would be a part of our marriage. We vowed to take a vacation each year. The memories of all the things we did together give me strength to move on. I miss my beautiful wife, but we lived our best life together.

If you are married, plan a vacation with your spouse because you can't afford not to. Memories are special, they keep you going when you have nothing else to lean on. I am glad we spent our best years traveling and experiencing the world together.

We started travelling modestly and eventually graduated to more exotic vacations. Our last trip in May of 2023 was in the Netherlands, what an adventure. Nicole saved the best for last; we caught the train from London to the Netherlands, then back to Paris. Can you believe we visited Disney Land in Paris. It was something to see and experience. Periodically I watch the videos on my phone to remember the good times that we shared.

Even when we didn't have a lot of money, holidays and entertaining is what we did. Our house was the place to visit on Thanksgiving and Christmas. Nicole and I have a difference in opinion regarding how we hosted a party. I believe if I invite you, just bring yourself and be prepared to take a plate. Nicole understood party etiquette; bring something when you come. This became a small tension point, but we managed to move beyond that discussion. The resolution, if you invite people make sure you buy the food yourself. I did finally understand how expensive it was to entertain although I never told her she was right.

Our good times centered on our son, Nick; we were very involved in his life, making sure he lived a comfortable childhood, free of stress and adult problems. Unfortunately, children today carry the frustrations of their parents. We wanted Nick to be a child and enjoy being a child.

Our good times also consisted of being the founding pastors of New Community church. Nicole never considered herself a pastor, but she was very responsible for the success of our ministry. Nicole did it all for the ministry and when she passed, we struggled to keep things running smooth because she worked in the spirit of excellence and did so many things well.

I never let people put pressure on her about being a first lady and she was able to carve out her own identity and be impactful in her own way. So many people comment that they wished they could have known Nicole before she passed. Nicole was the most generous person I ever met. Nicole was demanding of herself and wanted you to be the best version of yourself. She was like EF Hutton, when she spoke people listened.

The hard exterior was simply a barrier to keep the jokers away. Nicole was passionate about loving people unconditionally and leaving them better than when she met them. I remember when Nicole saw a pregnant waiter in a restaurant we frequently visited, she emptied her purse and gave her all the cash she had as she walked out of the restaurant. I remember Nicole going to Nordstrom to find a gift and cash for a waiter named Mona who served us at the Ritz-Carlton. Countless times I saw her bless people just because she could and wanted to. It was never to bring attention, but to be a blessing to others.

I never had to shop and if I mentioned I needed something, Amazon would arrive with a package within the next 48 hours. Our good times keep getting better as our marriage matured. I remember Covid, we were together all the time and loved every minute of it. I see so many men looking for reasons to not be at home, I enjoyed being at home with my wife.

I was very fortunate to marry my best friend. People must be able to grow together and understand their partner will change several times. The problem with most marriages is that they have immediate compatibility but are unable to make the adjustment when their partner evolves into a different version of the person that they feel in love with.

I believe what kept our marriage fresh was our ability to conversate.

When I first met Nicole, I would drive up to the pay phone and talk to her for up to three hours each night. We never ran out of conversation, because we genuinely wanted to know more about each other. After nearly 30 years of marriage, we still discovered new things about each other. I was madly in love with Nicole Gaynelle VanDyke. The amazing thing is she was super pretty when she woke up in the morning, no makeup was needed. I was and I still am in love. She made my temperature rise, just by looking at her. This will take a minute because my dedication to her is real. I know Nicole is no longer here, but the love is still real.

The good times continued because we both wanted to be the best version of ourselves for each other. Married couples take note, stop trying to control your spouse, let them become what God intended them to be. If you allow them to grow, you will find yourself always discovering more and more. Our marriage wasn't perfect, but it was genuine. We really liked and loved each other.

I was giddy when Nicole lost her hair from chemotherapy. I was giddy after the double mastectomy. It didn't matter about the changes she went through it was my job as her husband and protector to continue to love unconditionally. Nicole never called me fat boy after I put on a few extra pounds, she encouraged me to become a better person. I can remember Nicole buying me smaller clothes and she would say, eventually I would fit them. She was correct, fitness is part of my new normal. Nicole, after your passing you continue to be correct.

Finally, some of the best times we had were building the three new houses together. With each house we got what she wanted, and Nicole had the ability to put her finishing touch on each one. Each time we built I convinced Nicole this was the right move, then she went to work and made our house a home. Our last house she only lived in it for two years before taking ill.

I can honestly say she designed this big house for me. Every room I feel her presence and artistry. When I sit in the kitchen, I see her design and style. Our good times on earth together were amazing. I can honestly say, I was fulfilled as a husband. Nicole was the Proverbs 31 woman through and through.

One last thought, as I sit in the kitchen writing our love story with no music or television playing. I feel your presence all over this home. Thanks for looking out for me and leaving a comfortable place for me to live. You are the best Nicole. They broke the mold when God made you for me.

In Sickness and in Health

Traditional marriage vows

"I, _Anthony_____, take thee, __Nicole___, to be my wedded wife (husband), to have and to hold from this day forward, for better, for worse, for richer, for poorer, in sickness and in health, to love and to cherish, till death do us part."

On September 2, 1995, at 1pm I took those vows not fully understanding what they meant. I will start with the last few words my bride said to me, many people said the vows in sickness and health, Nicole stated, "Anthony you meant what you said, I know you love me because you keep loving me in sickness and never made me feel sick." Inside I was crying to know that Nicole recognized my commitment to take care of her. It was my pleasure to take care of God's daughter.

To many people Nicole's passing seemed sudden, but as I looked back over the past two decades, Nicole battled sickness many of those years. It all started with the pulmonary embolism that she had. A few years later, she was diagnosed with breast cancer, leading to a double mastectomy and other health challenges until the ovarian cancer overwhelmed her body. Notice I said her body because through the entire ordeal her mind remained sound and very aware of the battle she faced.

During the battles we lived life to the fullest. In retrospect Nicole knew at least a year before her earthly journey would end. Nicole was preparing me little by little, she would say things that didn't make sense then, now I understand.

The good times continued to roll, and we went to concerts and traveled with our mothers to the Bahamas. We continued to drive three hours to Liberty University football stadium to see the Liberty Flames march to victory each home game. We would take many vacations to the Washington DC area and stay at the Ritz Carlton and enjoy being pampered. We would walk in the morning in the neighborhood and take a dip in the pool before work. We both worked from home therefore we had the pleasure and privilege to eat every meal together, breakfast, lunch and dinner.

It was my pleasure to serve Nicole, and she taught me how to cook to her taste. We had a good arrangement. She would go grocery shopping, and I would cook the food. The last 5 months of her life she didn't have the energy to shop, and that became my responsibility to purchase the food and prepare it. Nicole wanted to keep up her responsibility of paying for the food so she would cashapp me money to cover the groceries. What a partner she continued to be despite the physical challenges she faced.

November 2023, things turned for the worse. I do believe Nicole stopped driving herself around August, and I knew something was going on when she didn't have the energy to drive anymore. I kept moving as if we had another 20 years on earth together. Nicole never shared with me how she really felt, because she didn't want to see me cry.

I remember early December crying and pleading with Nicole to eat, because I needed her strong and didn't want her to leave me in this world by myself, that wasn't our agreement. We did everything together and I do mean everything. We were inseparable because we really liked each other. It bothers me to see married people, fusing and tripping about things that don't matter. I would give anything just to spend another day on earth with my bride. God called my baby home, and I humbly accept his plan for her life. My name for Nicole was poo-de, when I said "poo-de" she would smile and be like a schoolgirl in love.

I can honestly say, the health challenges Nicole endured were our challenges. I would drive her to treatments, open my laptop and wait until she finished. Marriage is never an inconvenience when God is in the middle.

I knew the end was near when Nicole stopped calling family members and didn't want to have Thanksgiving and Christmas dinner. Ironically even if we wanted to host a family dinner, we couldn't because Nicole spent the holiday season in the hospital. We didn't tell our family, because we didn't want them to worry about us. I remember sleeping in those uncomfortable chairs and coming home every couple of days to shower and check the house. The hospital became our home. When

Nicole couldn't eat, I didn't either. I ate just enough to not get sick.

The journey she faced was a team effort and we were one to the end. The most difficult task I faced was the final days having to inject morphine so that she wouldn't feel the pain as her organs were shutting down. The final minutes of Nicole's life on earth, Nick and I held hands and told Nicole, "don't hold on for us, we will be ok, you can rest and be at peace."

Nick stepped out of the room, and I laid on the bed next to her as she continued to gasp for air. I remember a deep pulse and there was silence in the room. I immediately called Nick into the room, I remember him saying, "mom is resting now." There was a quiet that came over the house, and I felt God's presence had come and ushered his angel home.

In Conclusion

Sickness and health both looked and felt the same. When you love people unconditionally you do what you have to do. Time doesn't matter, cost doesn't matter, because the only person that matters other than God is the person you vowed to love in sickness and in health.

Nicole you will always be in my heart, you will never be forgotten. I will move on with my life, always keeping you in my heart. As a husband, I am fulfilled, you left no boxes unchecked. You were the perfect partner for me. I am amazed how two people with opposite beginnings became one over time. I was made for you and thank God you were made for me. This is not goodbye but see you later. I will make you proud. I promise to take care of your boys, Nick and Kingston, I got them. And let me not forget Lady "B" I got her.

Rest in peace, "poo-de".

Repairing Your Marriage

www.ingramcontent.com/pod-product-compliance
Lightning Source LLC
Chambersburg PA
CBHW081002140626
46546CB00018B/3066